I0020625

FORWARD/COMMENTARY

The National Institute of Standards and Technology (NIST) is a measurement standards laboratory, and a non-regulatory agency of the United States Department of Commerce. Its mission is to promote innovation and industrial competitiveness. Founded in 1901, as the National Bureau of Standards, NIST was formed with the mandate to provide standard weights and measures, and to serve as the national physical laboratory for the United States. With a world-class measurement and testing laboratory encompassing a wide range of areas of computer science, mathematics, statistics, and systems engineering, NIST's cybersecurity program supports its overall mission to promote U.S. innovation and industrial competitiveness by advancing measurement science, standards, and related technology through research and development in ways that enhance economic security and improve our quality of life.

The need for cybersecurity standards and best practices that address interoperability, usability and privacy has been shown to be critical for the nation. NIST's cybersecurity programs seek to enable greater development and application of practical, innovative security technologies and methodologies that enhance the country's ability to address current and future computer and information security challenges.

The cybersecurity publications produced by NIST cover a wide range of cybersecurity concepts that are carefully designed to work together to produce a holistic approach to cybersecurity primarily for government agencies and constitute the best practices used by industry. This holistic strategy to cybersecurity covers the gamut of security subjects from development of secure encryption standards for communication and storage of information while at rest to how best to recover from a cyber-attack.

Why buy a book you can download for free?

Some are available only in electronic media. Some online docs are missing pages or barely legible.

We at 4th Watch Books are former government employees, so we know how government employees actually use the standards. When a new standard is released, an engineer prints it out, punches holes and puts it in a 3-ring binder. While this is not a big deal for a 5 or 10-page document, many NIST documents are over 100 pages and printing a large document is a time-consuming effort. So, an engineer that's paid $75 an hour is spending hours simply printing out the tools needed to do the job. That's time that could be better spent doing engineering. We publish these documents so engineers can focus on what they were hired to do – engineering. It's much more cost-effective to just order the latest version from Amazon.com

If there is a standard you would like published, let us know. Our web site is Cybah.webplus.net

Please see the Cybersecurity Standards list at the end of this book.

CyberSecurity Standards Library™

Get a Complete Library of Over 300 Cybersecurity Standards on 1 Convenient DVD!

The **4th Watch CyberSecurity Standards Library** is a DVD disc that puts over 300 current and archived cybersecurity standards from NIST, DOD, DHS, CNSS and NERC at your fingertips! Many of these cybersecurity standards are hard to find and we included the current version and a previous version for many of them. The DVD includes four books written by Luis Ayala: **The Cyber Dictionary, Cybersecurity Standards, Cyber-Security Glossary of Building Hacks and Cyber-Attacks**, and **Cyber-Physical Attack Defenses: Preventing Damage to Buildings and Utilities**.

- ✓ DVD includes many Hard-to-find Cybersecurity Standards - some still in Draft.
- ✓ Docs are organized by source and listed numerically so each standard is easy to locate.
- ✓ The listing of standards on the DVD includes an abstract of the subject, and date issued.
- ✓ PDF format for use on PC, Mac, eReaders, or tablets.
- ✓ No need for WiFi / Internet.
- ✓ Save countless hours of searching and downloading.
- ✓ Carry in a briefcase - terrific for travel.

4th Watch Publishing is releasing the CyberSecurity Standards Library DVD to make it easier for you to access the tools you need to ensure the security of your computer networks and SCADA systems. We also publish many of these standards on demand so you don't need to waste valuable time searching for the latest version of a standard, printing hundreds of pages and punching holes so they can go in a three-ring binder. **Order on Amazon.com**

The DVD works on PC and Mac with the standards in PDF format. To view the CyberSecurity Standards Library on the DVD, a computer with a DVD drive is required. The most current version of your internet browser, at least 2GB of RAM, and current version of Adobe Reader is recommended. (Compatible browsers include Internet Explorer 8+, Mozilla Firefox 4+, Apple Safari 5+, Google Chrome 15+)

1

Draft NISTIR 8138

2

Vulnerability Description Ontology (VDO)

3

A Framework for Characterizing Vulnerabilities

4

5

6   Harold Booth
7   Christopher Turner
8

9

10

11

12

13

14

National Institute of
Standards and Technology
U.S. Department of Commerce

15

16

Draft NISTIR 8138

Vulnerability Description Ontology (VDO)

17

18

19

A Framework for Characterizing Vulnerabilities

20

21
22
23

Harold Booth
Computer Security Division
Information Technology Laboratory

24

25
26
27

Christopher Turner
Booz Allen Hamilton
McLean, VA

28

29

30

31

32

33

34

35

36

September 2016

37

38

39
40
41
42
43
44
45
46

U.S. Department of Commerce
Penny Pritzker, Secretary

National Institute of Standards and Technology
Willie May, Under Secretary of Commerce for Standards and Technology and Director

47 National Institute of Standards and Technology Internal Report 8138
48 45 pages (September 2016)

49

63 **Public comment period: *September 30, 2016* through *October 31, 2016***

64 All comments are subject to release under the Freedom of Information Act (FOIA).

65

66 National Institute of Standards and Technology
67 Attn: Computer Security Division, Information Technology Laboratory
68 100 Bureau Drive (Mail Stop 8930) Gaithersburg, MD 20899-8930
69 Email: nistir8138@nist.gov

70

71

72   **Reports on Computer Systems Technology**

73   The Information Technology Laboratory (ITL) at the National Institute of Standards and
74   Technology (NIST) promotes the U.S. economy and public welfare by providing technical
75   leadership for the Nation's measurement and standards infrastructure. ITL develops tests, test
76   methods, reference data, proof of concept implementations, and technical analyses to advance the
77   development and productive use of information technology. ITL's responsibilities include the
78   development of management, administrative, technical, and physical standards and guidelines for
79   the cost-effective security and privacy of other than national security-related information in federal
80   information systems.

81

82   **Abstract**

83   This document aims to describe a more effective and efficient methodology for characterizing
84   vulnerabilities found in various forms of software and hardware implementations including but
85   not limited to information technology systems, industrial control systems or medical devices to
86   assist in the vulnerability management process. The primary goal of the described methodology
87   is to enable automated analysis using metrics such as the Common Vulnerability Scoring System
88   (CVSS). Additional goals include establishing a baseline of the minimum information needed to
89   properly inform the vulnerability management process, and facilitating the sharing of
90   vulnerability information across language barriers.

91

92   **Keywords**

93   software defects; ontology; patching; taxonomy; vulnerabilities; vulnerability management

94

Acknowledgements

96 The authors, Harold Booth of the National Institute of Standards and Technology (NIST) and
97 Christopher Turner of Booz Allen Hamilton, wish to thank their colleagues who reviewed drafts
98 of this document and contributed to its technical content. The authors would like to acknowledge
99 Matthew Hansbury, Matthew Scola, and Steve Christey of the MITRE Corporation for their
100 insightful assistance in the development of this document.

Audience

102 This document is intended for anyone who participates in the vulnerability management process.
103 Possible stakeholders include security response teams of manufacturers who need to respond to
104 vulnerabilities discovered in their products, security researchers who wish to share vulnerability
105 information with manufacturers or other vulnerability coordination entities, system
106 administrators and/or owners who need to identify vulnerabilities in their systems and prioritize
107 their remediation, vulnerability discovery tool vendors, and vulnerability databases.

Note to Reviewers

109 This is the first draft of several anticipated drafts of a document intended to describe a
110 methodology for characterizing vulnerabilities. It is not intended to be complete at this time and
111 the authors do not expect that this draft reflects the full breadth and depth of the information
112 needed to fully automate the descriptions for vulnerabilities. Reviewers are asked to provide
113 feedback on terminology that is unclear, in conflict with established practice and are encouraged
114 to provide feedback and examples where the current draft falls short in enabling the description
115 of a vulnerability. To the extent that is reasonable and in keeping with the purpose of this
116 document (Section 1.1), future drafts will be produced attempting to incorporate this feedback
117 with the goal of improving the final version.

118 Questions and items of particular note have been highlighted to encourage feedback.

Trademark Information

120 CVE is a registered trademark of The MITRE Corporation.

121 All other registered trademarks or trademarks belong to their respective organizations.

122

123   **Document Conventions**

124   The key words "MUST", "MUST NOT", "REQUIRED", "SHALL", "SHALL NOT",

125   "SHOULD", "SHOULD NOT", "RECOMMENDED", "MAY", and "OPTIONAL" in this

126   report are to be interpreted as described in Request for Comment (RFC) 2119 [RFC2119]. When

127   these words appear in regular case, such as "should" or "may", they are not intended to be

128   interpreted as RFC 2119 key words.

Table of Contents

178 # 1   Introduction

179 When two or more groups share information, a common vocabulary is critical for success. The
180 cybersecurity landscape is relatively new and therefore is still in its infancy in developing these
181 shared vocabularies. The ontology described in this document is a fundamental building block in
182 developing that shared understanding for vulnerabilities among cybersecurity professionals. For
183 the purposes of this document a vulnerability is defined as any weakness in the computational
184 logic found in products or devices that could be exploited by a threat source [NISTIR 7298].
185
186 Managing these vulnerabilities within an organization is described as the vulnerability
187 management process. The vulnerability management process consists of identifying whether an
188 organization has endpoints containing the vulnerability, determining the exposure of the
189 vulnerability within the organization and evaluating the impact of successful exploitation of a
190 vulnerability within the context of the organization. An organization must determine whether the
191 exposure and impact of a specific vulnerability warrants a response and prioritize that response
192 among other critical activities. Organizations then need to make a similar decision for each
193 vulnerability. The analysis needed to inform the prioritization is currently a time-consuming,
194 manual process and is often based on reading security bulletins and vendor advisories which
195 sometimes provide incomplete or conflicting information.
196
197 This document defines a framework that improves upon this manual process by enabling a
198 mechanism to describe vulnerabilities in a machine consumable format. While this document
199 does not describe a particular format to encode the vulnerability data, it is expected other efforts
200 will use this document as a foundation for the creation of a machine processible format. The
201 format will enable automated tools to assist in the analysis process. In addition, consumers of
202 vulnerability information will be able use the vocabulary described in this framework to identify
203 missing information and encourage more complete and accurate vulnerability descriptions from
204 their providers. More complete and accurate descriptions will better facilitate the vulnerability
205 management process for organizations.
206
207 In addition to those responsible for an organization's vulnerability management function, other
208 stakeholders include:
209   • Security Researchers – who need to share and disclose vulnerability information to
210   vendors
211   • Software Publishers – who need to share and disclose vulnerability information to their
212   customers
213   • Vulnerability Coordinators – who need to share and disclose vulnerability information to
214   software publishers and to users of the affected software
215   • Vulnerability Information Services – that need to provide vulnerability information to the
216   consumers of their data, often performing additional analysis which can assist in the
217   prioritization of vulnerabilities for organizations
218
219 All of these stakeholders need a common language to describe and characterize vulnerabilities as
220 well as a way to express what information is needed to perform their activities. The framework
221 in this document intends to provide this common language and to provide a way for stakeholders
222 to describe required information.

223
224   **1.1   Purpose**

225   The purpose of this document is to create a more effective and efficient methodology within the
226   vulnerability management sphere that describes vulnerabilities in a universal manner.
227   Additionally, it enables automated scoring, improves the amount of detail that can be provided
228   about a vulnerability while minimizing the risk of the information being used to exploit the
229   vulnerability, and allows for better sharing of vulnerability information across language barriers.
230
231   **1.2   Methodology**

232   Any recommended concept or idea from stakeholders that align with the purpose stated in
233   Section 1.1 will be considered. Specifically the framework is focused on vulnerability
234   management and automating that process, and thus any additions or modifications will be made
235   to improve that use case.
236
237   This document is not intended to provide guidance on a particular implementation of syntax or
238   serialization, but to provide a framework that specifies available characteristics, valid values, and
239   relationships. If multiple serialization mechanisms are developed that adhere to this framework
240   they would hopefully be semantically interoperable.

241 **2   Overview**

242 The framework is composed of:

243 • **noun group** – a conceptual entity containing related noun group values;
244 • **noun group definition** – description of a noun group; what it is and how it is used;
245 • **usage** – each noun group is identified as:
246   ○ mandatory (M) – indicates a value for the noun group SHALL be provided,
247   ○ recommended (R) – indicates a value for the noun group SHOUD be provided,
248   ○ optional (O) – indicates a value for the noun group MAY be provided;
249 • **noun group values** – valid values are either chosen from an enumerated list of values
250   specific to each noun group or have an expected format. The format is composed of types
251   which are described in the ABNF notation of Section 2.1 with the type name represented
252   in italics as follows: *<typename>*;
253 • **noun group value definition** – description of a noun group value; what it is and how it is
254   used; and
255 • **relationships** – noun groups are related to each other through the allowed relationships
256   as described for the noun group. The cardinality of the relationship indicates whether
257   multiple values are permitted for the noun group. Noun group values may also have a
258   relationship to another noun group. Relationships will be represented in the following
259   format [<cardinality> <target noun group> " value/s " <usage> " be associated with "
260   (<origin noun group>/<origin noun group value>)].

261 When noun group names are referenced throughout this document they will appear in italics.

262 **2.1   Noun Group Value Types**

263 The following section describes the available types used to describe the expected format for noun
264 groups that have valid values that are not an enumerated list. The following uses Augmented
265 Backus–Naur Form (ABNF) as described in [RFC5234]. The formats for the valid values are
266 intended to describe the expected contents of the value and are not representative of any
267 particular syntax or serialization mechanism.

268   **Table 1 Valid Value Types**

source	= string
vulnerability-identifier	= namespace identifier
vulnerability-type	= namespace identifier
product-configuration	= 1*product-identifier / (namespace string)
product-identifier	= namespace identifier
namespace	= string

identifier	= string
string	= 1*VCHAR
Number	= 1*DIGIT

269

270 | **3   Noun Groups**

271 Noun groups are the core building block of the framework.

272 **3.1   Vulnerability**

A *Vulnerability* is any weakness in the computational logic found in products or devices that could be exploited by a threat source.

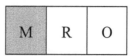

<vulnerability-identifier> Example: cve.mitre.org CVE-2015-1234	An identifier for a vulnerability supplied by a source. Examples include a knowledge base article number, patch number, a bug tracking datatbase identifier or a common identifier such as a Common Vulnerabilities and Exposures (CVE) identifier. CVE is a widely adopted identifier used across many organizations.

Relationships: *Scenario*, *Sector of Interest*, *Known Chain*, *Provenance*
- *One or many Scenario values shall be associated with Vulnerability.*
- *Zero or many Sector of Interest values may be associated with Vulnerability.*
- *Zero or many Known Chain values may be associated with Vulnerability.*
- *Zero or many Provenance values may be associated with Vulnerability.*

273
274

275   ### 3.2   Sector of Interest

Supplemental information identifying potential sectors or use cases where
the *Vulnerability* could have an impact.

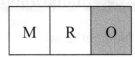

Industrial Control Systems[1]	The *Vulnerability* affects software that interfaces with manufacturing or production control systems.
Health Care	The *Vulnerability* is found within information systems that are related to health care. This includes both software whose purpose is to provide services specifically for health care, as well as medical devices.
Financial	The *Vulnerability* is found within software that relates to financial operations or activities.

Relationships: *Vulnerability*
- *Zero or many Sector of Interest values may be associated with Vulnerability.*

276

277   ### 3.3   Known Chain

An identifier for another known *Vulnerability* that can be used in
conjunction with the *Vulnerability* in question to achieve a different and
likely greater impact.

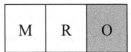

<vulnerability-identifier> Example: cve.mitre.org CVE-2015-1234	A central identifier for each vulnerability supplied by a source. Examples include a knowledge base article number, patch number, a bug tracking database identifier or a common identifier such as a CVE identifier.

Relationships: *Vulnerability*
- *Zero or many Known Chain values may be associated with Vulnerability.*

278

279

---

[1] The term 'industrial control system' is defined in NIST IR 7298 R2:
   http://nvlpubs.nist.gov/nistpubs/ir/2013/NIST.IR.7298r2.pdf

280   ### 3.4 Provenance
Representation of the source of the information for the related item.

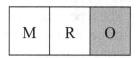

| *<source>* | The name of the source which provided the information related to the *Vulnerability*. |

Relationships: Vulnerability
- *Zero or many Provenance values may be associated with Vulnerability.*

281
282   ### 3.5 Scenario

A scenario is the placeholder to allow a description of the conditions surrounding the possible use of a vulnerability. *Vulnerability* must have a least one Scenario, with multiple possible *Scenario*s being common. A single *Vulnerability* can likely be exploited by many different approaches with possible varying impacts. For example a remote exploit could rely on user interaction to be downloaded, or a local attack could use the same vulnerability to obtain the same or similar impact.

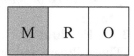

| <number> | A simple numerical identifier identifying this *Scenario* within the *Vulnerability*. |

Relationships: Vulnerability, Barriers, Context, Attack Theater, Product, Type
- *One or many Scenario values shall be associated with Vulnerability.*
- *Zero or many Barrier values should be associated with Scenario.*
- *One or many Context values shall be associated with Scenario.*
- *One and only one Attack Theater shall be associated with Scenario.*
- *Zero or many Product values may be associated with Scenario.*
- *Zero or many Type values may be associated with Scenario.*

283
284
285

286   ### 3.6   Type

The type, category, or weakness of the *Vulnerability*. When choosing a value, the most applicable types should be selected based on the type system used.

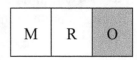

<vulnerability-type> Example: cwe.mitre.org CWE-123	An identifier of the vulnerability category, type or weakness. Examples of type systems include the Open Web Application Security Project (OWASP) Vulnerability Categories [OWASP-VULN] and the Common Weakness Enumeration (CWE) [CWE] which provide descriptions and names for various types of vulnerabilities.

Relationships: *Scenario*
- *Zero or many Type values may be associated with Scenario.*

287

288   ### 3.7   Product

The software and/or hardware configurations that are known to be vulnerable to exploitation of the *Vulnerability*. Different *Product* configurations can be associated with different *Scenarios* to allow for description of varying impacts and explotation mechanisms.

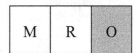

<product-configuration> Example: http://standards.iso.org/iso/19770/-2/2015 2001-06.com.acme_ACME_Application-1.01	A list of identifiers or an applicability language which allows for the description of the product configuration. Example product identifiers are Software Identifiers (SWID) as described in [ISO/IEC 19770-2:2015] and Common Platform Enumeration (CPE) names as described in [CPEN]. An example of an applicability language would be the CPE Applicability Language described in [CPEAL].

Relationships: *Scenario*
- *Zero or many Product values may be associated with Scenario.*

289

290

291   **3.8   Attack Theater**

Attack Theater is the area or place from which an attack must occur. Each separate theater represents varying levels of implied trust and attack surface.

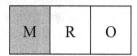

Remote	The exploit scenario requires that the attack occurs over the network stack; normally external to the target's internal network such as from the Internet. Common targets in the remote theater are public websites, Domain Name System (DNS) services, or web-browsers. *Noun-specific relationship: Remote Type* • *One and only one Remote Type value should be associated with Remote.*
Limited Remote	The exploit scenario requires that the attack can occur over layer 2 or layer 3 technologies, but a limitation exists either by the nature of the network communication or by range constraints. Examples of range constraints are *Cellular, Wireless, Bluetooth, Infrared,* or *Line-Of-Sight*. *Noun-specific relationship: Limited Remote Type* • *One and only one Limited Remote Type value should be associated with Limited Remote.*
Local	The exploit scenario requires that the attack can only occur after the adversary has logical local access to a device such as through a console, Remote Desktop Protocol (RDP), Secure Shell (SSH), or Telnet login.
Physical	The exploit scenario requires the attacker's physical presence at the target.

Relationships: Scenario
   • *One and only one Attack Theater value shall be associated with Scenario.*

292
293

294   **3.8.1 Remote Type**

Remote Type futher refines the *Remote* selection of the *Attack Theater* noun group to provide additional detail on where an adversary must be located. Selection of a *Remote Type* value will assist in determing the types of threats that can take advantage of the vulnerability.

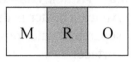

Internet	An attack is able to originate over the internet.
Intranet	The attack must be launched from within an organizations internal network that is shielded from direct access of the Internet. (Ex: A router is configured by default to only allow connections from the Intranet ports and not the WAN ports.) This also represents broadcast domains.
Local Network	An attacker must have access to a physical interface to the network, or collision domain.

Relationships: *Remote*
   • *One and only one Remote Type value should be associated with Remote.*

295

296   **3.8.2 Limited Remote Type**

Limited Remote Type futher refines the *Limited Remote* selection of the *Attack Theater* noun group to provide additional detail on where an adversary must be located. Selection of a *Limited Remote Type* value will assist in determing the types of threats that can take advantage of the vulnerability.

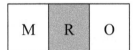

Cellular	The attack must be launched from a cellular network.
Wireless	The attack must be launched from a wireless (802.11x) network.
Bluetooth	The attack must be launched relying on a Bluetooth communication channel.
Infrared	The attack must be launched relying on an Infrared communication channel.
Line-of-Sight	The attack must be launched using a Line-of-Sight system such as ocular.

Relationships: *Limited Remote*
   • *One and only one Limited Remote Type value should be associated with Limited Remote.*

297

298

299   **3.9   Barrier**

Any characteristic inherent in the vulnerability that could impede the adversary from achieving successful exploitation. A barrier increases the difficulty an attacker faces when attempting to execute an exploit for the vulnerability.

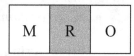

Social Engineering	The exploit scenario requires that an attacker perform some type of social engineering to achieve a successful exploit attempt. Typically, an attacker convinces a victim into interacting with a malicious resource. *Noun-specific relationship: Engineering Method, Victim Type* • *One or many Engineering Method values should be associated with Social Engineering.* • *Zero or one Victim Type values should be associated with Social Engineering.*
Race Condition	The exploit scenario includes requiring an attacker to take advantage of a race condition. *Noun-specific relationship: Race Condition Type* • *One and only one Race Condition Type value should be associated with Race Condition.*
Specialized Condition	The exploit scenario requires specific, non-default configuration settings within the vulnerable software. For example the use of a non-standard port for a networked service like ssh.
Environmental Condition	The exploit scenario requires an environmental condition external to the vulnerable software that is not necessarily related to the vulnerable software itself. A congested network would be an example of an environmental condition.
Precondition Required	Information about the target is necessary in order to exploit the vulnerability on a specific target. For example the hostname of the device may necessary in order to exploit the vulnerability on that device.
Privilege Required	The exploit scenario requires an attacker to have certain privileges prior to successful exploitation attempts. *Noun-specific relationship: Privilege Information* • *Zero or one Privilege Information values should be associated with Privilege Required.* *Noun-specific relationship: Privilege Level* • *One and only one Privilege Level value should be associated with Privilege Required.* *Noun-specific relationship: Context* • *One and only one Context value should be associated with Privilege Required.*

Relationships: <u>*Scenario*</u>
  • *Zero or many Barrier values should be associated with Scenario.*

300

301 **3.9.1 Engineering Method**

The method or mechanism used to manipulate a user into interacting with a malicious resource.

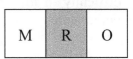

Malicious Link	A URL or hyperlink that has been crafted in a way that causes a target program or website to operate in an unintended fashion
Malicious File	A file that has been crafted in a way that causes a target program to operate in an unintended fashion
Malicious Website Content	A website that has been crafted in a way that causes a target program to operate in an unintended fashion or is used to simulate a site that the target user trusts.
Malicious Application	An application that has been modified or crafted to perform operations that are unintended

Relationships: <u>*Social Engineering*</u>
  • *One or many Engineering Method values should be associated with Social Engineering.*

302
303

304 **3.9.2 Victim Type**

When a user is targeted through the use of *Social Engineering* the *Victim Type* is used to describe the possible *Privilege Level* values along with the *Context* of those privileges. The level of privilege the target has should be reflected in the *Logical Impact* and *Physical Impact* values selected.

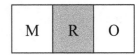

<number>	A simple numerical identifier to identify this instance of a victim for the *Scenario*.

Relationships: <u>*Social Engineering*</u>, <u>*Context*</u>, <u>*Privilege Level*</u>
  • *Zero or one Victim Type instances should be associated with Social Engineering.*
  • *One and only one Context value should be associated with Victim Type.*
  • *One and only one Privilege Level value should be associated with Victim Type.*

305

306   ### 3.9.3   Race Condition Type

Race Condition Type further refines the *Race Condition* selection of the *Barrier* noun group to provide additional detail on the level of likely control an adversary has to trigger the vulnerable race condition. Note that this is only a description of how much control an attacker has over the inputs involved in the race condition and not an indication of the reproducibility of triggering the race condition itself.

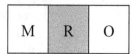

No Control	An attacker has no control over how the race condition will be triggered. The attacker must be fortunate to encounter the race condition.
Partial Control	An attacker is able to start one or more of the inputs which take part in the race condition but does not have control over all inputs. For example a vulnerability exists in the processing of a particular type of input on the intial start-up of a device and an attacker must supply that input during the period when the device is starting up and the attacker has no control over when the device starts up.
Full Control	An attacker is able to routinely start all inputs which will trigger the race condition.

Relationships: *Race Condition*

- *One and only one Race Condition Type value should be associated with Race Condition.*

307
308
309   ### 3.9.4   Privilege Information

Extra information regarding the *Privilege Required* barrier. This includes factors about privileges required before an attack is launched that can alter the attack's complexity.

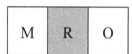

Multiple Authentication	Exploiting the vulnerability requires that the attacker authenticate two or more times, even if the same credentials are used each time. An example is an attacker authenticating to an operating system in addition to providing credentials to access an application hosted on that system.

Relationships: *Privilege Required*

- *Zero or one Privilege Information values should be associated with Privilege Required.*

310
311

312   ### 3.9.5   Privilege Level

Abstraction to assist in capturing relative privilege levels. The abstraction
is only for the sake of discussing the vulnerability and is not intended to
communicate the actual granular privileges that exist in most information
system environments.

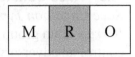

Anonymous	No privileges required. NOTE: Is this a needed value? Should the lack of an associated *Privilege Level* infer this? Or does the absence of a *Privilege Level* indicate a lack of knowledge?
User	Representative of a generic or basic user.
Privileged	Representative of something more than a base user, but not the full control of an Administrator
Administrator	Representative of when the privilege allows complete or nearly complete access to the context. Common terms include Admin, Administrator, Root, System or Kernel.
Generic Trust	This level is for applications or software packages that allow public account creation. Meaning that anyone who has access to the software has the abilility to create an account and access basic functionality.

Relationships: *Privilege Required*, *Privilege Escalation*
  - *One and only one Privilege Level value should be associated with Privilege Required.*
  - *One and only one Privilege level value should be associated with Privilege Escalation.*

313

314
315   ### 3.10 Context

The entity where the impacts are realized from successful exploitation of a
security vulnerability. Different impacts can be realized by multiple
contexts from multiple scenarios.

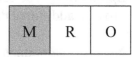

Hypervisor	A program or operating system that coordinates the sharing of hardware resources for multiple operating systems. Each guest operating system appears to have its own processor, memory, and other resources to itself. However, the hypervisor is controlling the shared hardware resources, allocating what is needed to each operating system as necessary, and isolating the guest operating systems from each other.
Firmware	Stored software that is considered to be built-in to a device. This is most commonly seen within embedded devices, routers, firewalls, BIOS and UEFI.
Host OS	An operating system running as the foundation layer for other software applications. This is intended to be used when the Hypervisor context **is not** applicable, otherwise Guest OS should be used.
Guest OS	An operating system running as the foundation layer for other software applications. This is intended to be used when the Hypervisor context **is** applicable, otherwise Host OS should be used.
Application	A program designed and implemented to accomplish a specific task. Applications can run on or within operating systems, firmware or other applications. *Noun-specific relationship: Application Type* • *Zero or more Application Type values should be associated with Application.*
Channel	The logical communication medium that is being used between other contexts. Channel is intended to be used when a protocol or cipher suite has a flaw inherently as opposed to an implementation issue. Examples would be failures of sufficient entropy in the cipher text or cryptographic key strength.
Physical Hardware	The actual physical hardware such as the logic gates within processors, the sectors of a disk or cells within memory.

Relationships: Entity Role, Impact Method, Mitigation, Privilege Required, Victim Type
   • *Zero or many Entity Role values should be associated with Context.*
   • *One or many Impact Method values shall be associated with Context.*
   • *Zero or many Mitigation values may be associated with Context.*
   • *One and only one Context value should be associated with Privilege Required.*
   • *One and only one Context value should be associated with Victim Type.*

316
317

318   **3.11 Application Type**

Application Type further refines the *Application* noun group value to provide additional detail on the category or type of application.

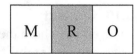

NOTE: The noun group values are not exhaustive and are intended to be illustrative of the types of values. Feedback on whether this is needed or desired is requested.

| Web Server | An application which provides general web server functions. |
| Database | An application which provide database functions. |

Relationships: Application
* *Zero or many Application Type values should be associated with Application.*

319

320   **3.12 Entity Role**

Describes the role an associated *Context* performs in the vulnerability scenario being described.

Vulnerable	Associated *Context* contains the *Vulnerability*
Primary Authorization	Associated *Context* is the main or initial authorization scope of the vulnerability scenario. See section 2.2 in [CVSSV3] for a full description of authorization scope.
Secondary Authorization	Associated *Context* is the secondary authorization scope of the vulnerability scenario. See section 2.2 in [CVSSV3] for a full description of authorization scope.

Relationships: Context
* *One or many Entity Role values shall be associated with Context.*

321

322   **3.13 Mitigation**

Describes protection mechanisms that may limit the impact or actions that can be taken even if the vulnerability is able to be exploited. These mechanisms are often part of the system in which the product is deployed or are inherent in how the product is used.

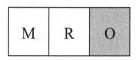

NOTE: This noun group is intended to capture situations where a vulnerability exists but the manner in which the product is used mitigates the vulnerability. Is this useful? Are the noun group values the right type of thing to capture?

ASLR	Some form of Address space layout randomization (ASLR) is in use.
Multi-Factor Authentication	Some form of Multi-Factor Authentication is required to access the product.
Sandboxed	The product is deployed within a sandbox.
HPKP/HSTS	HTTP Public Key Pinning (HPKP) or HTTP Strict Transport Security (HSTS) is in use.
Physical Security	Some form of physical security is in place that would mitigate this vulnerability.

Relationships: Context
- *Zero or many Mitigation values may be associated with Context.*

323
324

325   **3.14 Impact Method**

A description of the method used to exploit a vulnerability providing some additional information on the impact of exploitation.

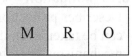

NOTE: Are there additional Noun Group values?

Context Escape	The *Vulnerability* allows an adversary to exploit a trust mechanism by breaking out of a sandbox and into another workspace. This *Impact Method* noun group value is intended to be associated with the *Context* that has been escaped. *Noun-specific relationship: Context* • *One and only one Context value shall be associated with Context Escape. The association denotes where a sandbox breakout originated.*
Trust Failure	Exploitation of the *Vulnerability* takes advantage of an assumed trust relationship leading to unexpected impacts. Examples include failures of inherent trust, failure to verify a communicator, or the content being transmitted. *Noun-specific Relationship: Trust Failure Type* • *One or many Trust Failure Type values should be associated with Trust Failure.*
Authentication Bypass	Exploitation of the *Vulnerability* takes advantage of a failure to identify the adversary properly, directly leading to additional access or permissions.
Man-in-the-Middle	The exploit scenario requires that an adversary perform a Man-in-the-Middle (MitM) attack. MitM attacks involve an adversary positioning themselves inside a communication channel between two or more parties. This is usually accomplished by exploiting a trust mechanism and tricking both ends of the communication channel into believing that they are communicating with the intended party. Once successfully injected into a communication channel, the MitM is capable of sensitive data disclosure, modification of data being transmitted, transmission of false data to either party (impersonation) or denial of communication to either party.
Code Execution	Exploitation of the *Vulnerability* allows an adversary to execute unauthorized code, causing an impact to a *Context*.

Relationships: Context, Logical Impact, Physical Impact
- *One or many Impact Methods shall be associated with Context*
- *One or many Logical Impacts shall be associated with Impact Method*
- *Zero or many Physical Impacts should be associated with Impact Method*

326
327

328   **3.14.1 Trust Failure Type**

A refinement to describe the type of failure in the associated *Context* which exposed the vulnerability.

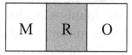

Failure to verify receiver	The *Context* failed to ensure the entity on the receiving end of the communication is the intended entity.
Failure to verify transmitter	The *Context* failed to ensure the entity on the transmitting end of the communication is the intended entity.
Failure to verify content	The *Context* failed to ensure the content supplied is properly formatted and sanitized.
Failure to establish trust	The *Context* failed to verify the input originated from a trusted source, in other words a check is missing or non-existent.

Relationships: Trust Failure

- *One or many Trust Failure Type of Trust values should be associated with Trust Failure.*

329

330   **3.15 Logical Impact**
A description of the possible impacts to the *Context* that a successful
exploitation of the *Vulnerability* can have. The same *Vulnerability* can
have multiple and different *Logical Impact* noun group values across
different *Context* or *Scenario* instances.

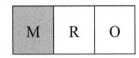

Write (Direct)	The *Vulnerability* allows an adversary to cause a breach in the integrity of the *Context* through unauthorized modification or addition of data.
Read (Direct)	The *Vulnerability* allows an adversary to cause a breach of confidentiality by gaining unauthorized access to data in the *Context*.
Resource Removal (Data)	The *Vulnerability* allows an adversary to perform an unauthorized removal (deletion) of data from a resource in the *Context*.
Service Interrupt	The *Vulnerability* allows an adversary to cause an unauthorized loss of availability by temporarily or permanently disabling all or a portion of the *Context*. *Noun-specific relationship: Service Interrupt Type* • *One or many Service Interrupt Type values should be associated with Service Interrupt.*
Indirect Disclosure	The *Vulnerability* allows an adversary to learn information about the *Context*, but the knowledge gained is not from a direct read operation. Examples include but are not limited to discovering memory locations protected by ASLR, information from side-channel attacks, or information gained from traffic analysis.
Privilege Escalation	The *Vulnerability* allows an adversary to gain a level of privilege that was not intended. Unlike the other Logical Impact noun group values, *Privilege Escalation* is intended to represent that anything the *Privilege Level* acquired can do, can be done by the adversary. If an adversary is able to only accomplish a subset of the other *Logical Impact* noun group values, that subset MUST be associated to the *Context* as well. Otherwise, all other *Logical Impact* noun group values are assumed. *Noun-specific relationship: Privilege Level* • *One and only one Privilege level value should be associated with Privilege Escalation.*

Relationships: Impact Method, Location, Scope
- *One or many Logical Impact values shall be associated with Impact Method*
- *Zero or many Location values may be associated with Logical Impact*
- *One and only one Scope value shall be associated with Logical Impact*

331

332   **3.15.1 Service Interrupt Type**

Additional information to describe the nature and type of service
interruption possible through the exploitation of a *Vulnerability*. Both
Service Interrupt Type and *Scope* noun group values should be applied
where applicable.

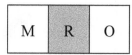

Shutdown	The service interruption results in the *Context* shutting down
Reboot	The service interruption results in the *Context* powering off, but starting back up immediately.
Hang	The service interruption results in the *Context* being stuck at a certain point and unable to continue function
Panic	The service interruption results in the *Context* crashing
Unrecoverable	The service interruption results in a complete and unrecoverable loss of the *Context* but is non-physical in nature. For example the corruption of the firmware on a hardware device with no possibility of reload.

Relationships: Service Interrupt

- *One or many Service Interrupt Type values should be associated with Service Interrupt.*

333

334   **3.15.2 Location**

A refinement to the Logical Impact noun group values designating the specific area or location impacted. Serves as supplemental information for the overall *Vulnerability* description.

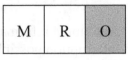

Memory	The *Logical Impact* is able to occur within memory
File System	The *Logical Impact* is able to occur within the file system
Network Traffic	The *Logical Impact* is able to occur within network traffic

Relationships: Logical Impact
- *Zero or many Location values may be associated with Logical Impact*

335
336   **3.16 Physical Impact**

Used when exploitation of the *Vulnerability* could result in a tangible impact to the physical device or machinery controlled by or through the *Context*, or the surrounding environment, which could be other nearby devices, machinery or people.

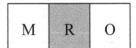

Physical Resource Consumption	An exploit of the *Vulnerability* could cause excessive physical resource consumption resulting in a tangible cost. *Noun-specific relationship: Physical Consumption Type* • *One or many Physical Consumption Type values must be associated with Physical Resource Consumption.*
Property Damage	An exploit of the *Vulnerability* could result in physical damage to the device or surrounding environment.
Human Injury	An exploit of the *Vulnerability* could result in injury to users or nearby individuals. *Noun-specific relationship: Human Injury Level* • *One and only one Human Injury Level value should be associated with Human Injury.*

Relationships: Impact Method, Scope
- *One and only one Scope value shall be associated with Physical Impact*
- *Zero or many Physical Impact values should be associated with Impact Method*

337

338   **3.16.1 Physical Consumption Type**

The *Vulnerability* allows for consumption of resources outside the digital realm. This consumption could lead to wear and tear on the hardware or financial implications from usage.

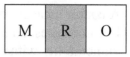

Electricity	Exploitation of the *Vulnerability* enables excessive electricity usage
Water	Exploitation of the *Vulnerability* enables excessive water usage
Assets	Exploitation of the *Vulnerability* enables excessive use of an asset. The excessive use could decrease the usable lifetime of the asset or unnecessarily consume fuel.

Relationships: *Physical Resource Consumption*
- *One or many Physical Consumption Type values should be associated with Physical Resource Consumption.*

339

340   **3.16.2 Human Injury Level**

A description of the possible impacts to any human as a result of exploitation of the *Vulnerability*. Descriptions below are based on Table D.3 in [ISO/IEC 14971:2007].

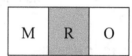

Negligible	Inconvenience or temporary discomfort
Minor	Temporary injury or impairment not requiring professional medical intervention
Serious	Injury or impairment requiring professional medical intervention
Critical	Permanent impairment or life-threatening injury
Catastrophic	Death

Relationships: *Human Injury*
- *One and only one Human Injury Level value should be associated with Human Injury.*

341

23

342   **3.17 Scope**

A coarse measure of the level of impact an exploit could have on a target. 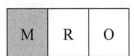 In some cases, an impact has no constraints at all. An example of this is a vulnerability with a 'Read (Direct)' *Logical Impact* association in which the adversary has access to the entire system, and thus has no constraints. In other cases, an *Impact* might have some constraints in place. An example of this is 'Write (Direct) *Impact* where the attacker is able to modify resources only accessible by the user.

Limited	There are restrictions to the associated impact *Noun-specific relationship: Criticality* • *One and only one Criticality value shall be associated with Limited*
Unlimited	There are no restrictions to the associated impact

Relationships: Logical Impact, Physical Impact
  • *One and only one Scope value shall be associated with Logical Impact*
  • *One and only one Scope value shall be associated with Physical Impact*

343

344   **3.18 Criticality**

A measure of the relative importance of the associated *Scope*. This noun  group is only relevant when the *Scope* has a value of 'Limited'. When *Scope* is 'Limited', *Criticality* must be used in order to provide additional information about its importance.

Criticality must be considered in concert with the *Context* to which it is associated. That is, for a given *Context* (such as *Guest OS* or *Application*), the *Criticality* should reflect how significant an associated impact could be for the specific *Context*. An impact in a *'Guest OS' Context* may be of lower significance than the same impact in a *'Host OS' Context* and should be reflected accordingly by its associated *Criticality*.

Low	The impact is relatively insignificant.
High	The impact is relatively significant.

Relationships: Scope
  • *One and only one Criticality value shall be associated with Limited*

345

346 ## 4   Conclusion

347 This first draft of this document provides one possible framework for describing vulnerabilities.
348 It is expected that comments on this draft will significantly influence the framework and as the
349 document evolves it will reflect a broad consensus. Future drafts will continue to refine all
350 aspects of the framework including alternative noun groups, noun group values, or even a
351 wholesale change in approach if necessary.
352

353 **Appendix A—Example Usage**

354 This appendix is intended to be an informative section describing one way on how to apply the framework to task of
355 describing a vulnerability. This section will continue to be updated as the framework evolves.

CVE-2012-1516
VMware host memory overwrite vulnerability (data pointers)
Due to a flaw in the handler function for RPC commands, it is possible to manipulate data pointers within the
VMX process. This vulnerability may allow a guest user to crash the VMX process or potentially execute code on
the host.

Vulnerability: cve.mitre.org CVE-2012-1516

Provenance: http://www.vmware.com/security/advisories/VMSA-2012-0009.html	
Scenario: 1	The first scenario
Product: cpe.nist.gov cpe:2.3:a:vmware:esx:4.0:*:*:*:*:*:*:* cpe:2.3:a:vmware:esx:4.1:*:*:*:*:*:*:* cpe:2.3:a:vmware:esx:3.5:*:*:*:*:*:*:* cpe:2.3:a:vmware:esxi:4.0:*:*:*:*:*:*:* cpe:2.3:a:vmware:esxi:4.1:*:*:*:*:*:*:* cpe:2.3:a:vmware:esxi:3.5:*:*:*:*:*:*:*	Scenario 1 is in relation to the bare metal hypervisor products
Attack Theater: Remote Remote Type: Intranet	Malformed RPC commands are sent from the Guest OS to the Hypervisor

Barrier: Privilege Required
  Privilege Level: User
   Relating to Context: GuestOS
	The attacker must first have user access to a GuestOS to launch the attack

Context: GuestOS	One of the *Contexts* with recognized impacts due to the vulnerability
Entity Role: Primary Authorization	The GuestOS is where the attack is launched and represents the first authorization scope
Impact Method: Code Execution	Direct result of failed code execution would be a crash of the Hypervisor and inherent crash of the GuestOS. Since the GuestOS would be completely taken offline, the criticality is listed as High

Logical Impact: Service Interrupt
  Location: Memory
  Service Interrupt Type: Panic
   Scope: Limited
   Criticality: High	

Context: Hypervisor	Another *Context* with recognized impacts due to the vulnerability
Entity Role: Vulnerable	Based on the description the Hypervisor is what is considered vulnerable.
Entity Roles Secondary Authorization	The hypervisor represents an authorization boundary that is different from the GuestOS
Impact Method: Trust Failure Trust Failure Type: Failure to Verify Content Impact Method: Code Execution	The Hypervisor fails to ensure that the data is in a form that prevents unintended *Code Execution*

Logical Impact: Read(Direct)
  Scope: Limited
   Criticality: High
Logical Impact: Write(Direct)
  Scope: Limited
   Criticality: High
Logical Impact: Service Interrupt
	The information supplied does not explicitly explain the extent of the code execution which results in each plausible logical impact being enumerated. If limitations to this code execution existed, it should be reflected in these *Logical Impacts*.

Scope: Limited
  Criticality: High
Logical Impact: Resource Removal(Data)
  Scope: Limited
  Criticality: High	

Scenario: 2	The second scenario
Product: cpe.nist.gov cpe:2.3:a:vmware:workstation:7.1.5:*:*:*:*:*:*:* cpe:2.3:a:vmware:player:3.1.6:*:*:*:*:*:*:*	Scenario 2 is in relation to application based Hypervisors
Attack Theater: Local	Malformed RPC commands are sent from the Guest OS to the Hypervisor, but by nature of the product everything is local to the HostOS where everything has been installed.

Barrier: Privilege Required
  Privilege Level: User
    Relating to Context: GuestOS
	The attacker must first have user access to a GuestOS to launch the attack

Context: GuestOS	One of the *Contexts* with recognized impacts due to the vulnerability
Entity Role: Primary Authorization	The GuestOS is where the attack is launched and represents the first authorization scope
Impact Method: Code Execution	Direct result of failed code execution would be a crash of the Hypervisor and inherent crash of the GuestOS. Since the GuestOS would be completely taken offline, the criticality is listed as High

Logical Impact: Service Interrupt
  Location: Memory
  Service Interrupt Type: Panic
    Scope: Limited
    Criticality: High	

Context: Hypervisor	Another *Context* with recognized impacts due to the vulnerability
Entity Role: Vulnerable	Based on the description the Hypervisor is what is considered vulnerable.
Entity Role: Secondary Authorization	The hypervisor represents an authorization boundary that is different from the GuestOS
Impact Method: Trust Failure Trust Failure Type: Failure to Verify Content Impact Method: Code Execution	The Hypervisor fails to ensure that the data is in a form that prevents unintended Code Execution

Logical Impact: Read(Direct)
  Scope: Limited
  Criticality: High
Logical Impact: Write(Direct)
  Scope: Limited
  Criticality: High
Logical Impact: Service Interrupt
  Scope: Limited
  Criticality: High
Logical Impact: Resource Removal(Data)
  Scope: Limited
  Criticality: High
	The information supplied does not explicitly explain the extent of the code execution which results in each plausible logical impact being enumerated. If limitations to this code execution existed, it should be reflected in these Logical Impacts.

356
357

CVE-2015-1863

A vulnerability was found in how wpa_supplicant uses SSID information parsed from management frames that create or update P2P peer entries (e.g., Probe Response frame or number of P2P Public Action frames). SSID field has valid length range of 0-32 octets. However, it is transmitted in an element that has a 8-bit length field and potential maximum payload length of 255 octets. wpa_supplicant was not sufficiently verifying the payload length on one of the code paths using the SSID received from a peer device.

This can result in copying arbitrary data from an attacker to a fixed length buffer of 32 bytes (i.e., a possible overflow of up to 223 bytes). The SSID buffer is within struct p2p_device that is allocated from heap. The overflow can override couple of variables in the struct, including a pointer that gets freed. In addition about 150 bytes (the exact length depending on architecture) can be written beyond the end of the heap allocation.

This could result in corrupted state in heap, unexpected program behavior due to corrupted P2P peer device information, denial of service due to wpa_supplicant process crash, exposure of memory contents during GO Negotiation, and potentially arbitrary code execution.

Vulnerability: cve.mitre.org CVE-2015-1863

Provenance: http://w1.fi/security/2015-1/wpa_supplicant-p2p-ssid-overflow.txt	
Scenario: 1	The first scenario
Type: cve.mitre.org CWE-119	
Product: cpe.nist.gov cpe:2.3:a:w1.fi:wpa_supplicant:1.0 cpe:2.3:a:w1.fi:wpa_supplicant:1.1 cpe:2.3:a:w1.fi:wpa_supplicant:2.0 cpe:2.3:a:w1.fi:wpa_supplicant:2.1 cpe:2.3:a:w1.fi:wpa_supplicant:2.2 cpe:2.3:a:w1.fi:wpa_supplicant:2.3 cpe:2.3:a:w1.fi:wpa_supplicant:2.4	
Attack Theater: Limited Remote Remote Type: Wireless	The attacker must be within radio range
Barrier: Specialized Condition	CONFIG_P2P build option must be enabled
Context: Application	
Entity Role: Primary Authorization Entity Role: Vulnerable	The Application is the only authorization scope
Impact Method: Trust Failure Trust Failure Type: Failure to Verify Content Impact Method: Code Execution	The Code Execution can lead to limited read of memory, crash of the process or unexplored other outcomes.

Logical Impact: Service Interrupt
  Service Interrupt Type: Panic
    Scope: Limited
    Criticality: High
Logical Impact: Read(Direct)
  Location: Memory
  Scope: Limited
    Criticality: Low
Logical Impact: Write(Direct)
  Scope: Limited
    Criticality: High	

358
359

CVE-2015-5611

Unspecified vulnerability in Uconnect before 15.26.1, as used in certain Fiat Chrysler Automobiles (FCA) from 2013 to 2015 models, allows remote attackers in the same cellular network to control vehicle movement, cause human harm or physical damage, or modify dashboard settings via vectors related to modification of entertainment-system firmware and access of the CAN bus due to insufficient "Radio security protection," as demonstrated on a 2014 Jeep Cherokee Limited FWD.

Vulnerability: cve.mitre.org CVE-2015-1863

Provenance: http://illmatics.com/Remote%20Car%20Hacking.pdf	
Scenario: 1	The first scenario
Product: cpe.nist.gov cpe:2.3:a:fca:uconnect:15.26.1:*:*:*:*:*:*:*	
Attack Theater: Limited Remote Limited Remote Type: Cellular	The attacker must be on the same cellular network as the target
Context: Application	
Entity Role: Primary Authorization Entity Role: Vulnerable	The Application is the only authorization scope

Impact Method: Trust Failure
    Trust Failure Type: Failure of Inherent Trust
Impact Method: Code Execution
Logical Impact: Read(Direct)
    Scope: Limited
     Criticality: High
Logical Impact: Write(Direct)
    Scope: Limited
     Criticality: High
 	
Logical Impact: Service Interrupt
 	
    Scope: Unlimited
 	
Logical Impact: Resource Removal (Data)
    Scope: Limited
     Criticality: High
Physical Impact: Human Injury
    Human Injury Type: Critical
Physical Impact: Property Damage
    Scope: Unlimited
	Anonymous access to the D-bus service allows execution of arbitrary code. This code execution allows modification of lateral internal devices, bricking of chipset or issuing of basic commands. Once these actions are taken, an attacker can control most aspects of the vehicle such as AC, radio and even physical functions such as steering and braking.

360
361

29

CVE-2014-8606
Directory traversal vulnerability in the XCloner plugin 3.1.1 for WordPress and 3.5.1 for Joomla! allows remote administrators to read arbitrary files via a .. (dot dot) in the file parameter in a json_return action in the xcloner_show page to wp-admin/admin-ajax.php.

Vulnerability: cve.mitre.org CVE-2014-8606

Provenance: http://www.vapid.dhs.org/advisories/wordpress/plugins/Xcloner-v3.1.1/	
Scenario: 1	
Type: cve.mitre.org CWE-22	
Products: cpe.nist.gov cpe:2.3:a:xcloner:xcloner:3.1.1:*:*:*:*:wordpress:*:* cpe:2.3:a:xcloner:xcloner:3.5.1:*:*:*:*:joomla\!:*:*	
Attack Theater: Remote	The attack can be launched from the Internet
Remote Type: Internet	
Barriers: Privilege Required	The attacker is required to have administrator rights within the application prior to exploit
Privilege Level: Administrator	
Relating to Context: Application	
Context: Application	
Entity Roles: Primary Authorization Entity Roles: Vulnerable	The Application is the initial authorization scope
Impact Method: Trust Failure Trust Failure Type: Failure to Verify Content	The attack can read files on the HostOS, which implies some file read realative to the Application as well. Since the user is already an administrator of the application, the criticality is Low

Logical Impact: Read(Direct)
  Scope: Limited
    Criticality: Low	

Context: HostOS	
Entity Roles: Secondary Authorization	
Impact Method: Code Execution	

Logical Impact: Read(Direct)
  Scope: Limited
    Criticality: High
	The attack can read files on the HostOS. Since the file in the example supplied is etc/passwd the criticality can be High.

362

CVE-2015-3459

The communication module on the Hospira LifeCare PCA Infusion System before 7.0 does not require authentication for root TELNET sessions, which allows remote attackers to modify the pump configuration via unspecified commands.

Vulnerability: cve.mitre.org CVE-2015-3459	
Provenance: http://www.fda.gov/MedicalDevices/Safety/AlertsandNotices/ucm446809.htm	
Sector of Interest: Health Care	
Scenario: 1	The first scenario
Type: cve.mitre.org CWE-306	The attack takes advantage of a lack of authentication on the telnet service
Product: cpe.nist.gov cpe:2.3:o:hospira:lifecare_pcainfusion_firmware:5.0:*:*:*:*:*:*:*	
Attack Theater: Remote Remote Type: Internet	The attack can be launched from the internet
Context: Host OS	The vulnerability is in the underlying host OS that provides the remote programming capability for the pump
Entity Role: Primary Authorization Entity Role: Vulnerable	The Host OS is the initial authorization scope and is also the vulnerable Context
Impact Method: Trust Failure Trust Failure Type: Failure of Inherent Trust Impact Method: Authorization Bypass	The attack involves remotely taking advantage of the lack of authentifcaiton during use of telnet on the host OS. Since there is no authorization, this is a exploitation of a trust relationship. This can lead to unspecified types of service interruption and the ability to view and modify the pump's configuration.

Logical Impact: Service Interrupt
  Scope: Unlimited
Logical Impact: Read(Direct)
  Location: File System
  Scope: Unlimited
Logical Impact: Write(Direct)
  Location: FileSystem
  Scope: Unlimited	

Physical Impact: Human Injury	The attack can result in the delivery of an incorrect, and possible deadly level of medicine

363

364

31

365
366   **Appendix B—Conversion to descriptive text (English)**

367   This appendix will include an informative demonstration of how to convert the framework
368   selections and values into English text. Future drafts will include this information.

369 **Appendix C—Mapping VDO representations to CVSS Scores**

370 One of the motivations for the VDO is to assist in the automation of CVSS scores. Currently the NVD is responsible
371 for manually consolidating public records and performing analysis on the information available. One of the
372 challenges of performing the analysis is that information supplied is usually lacking in sufficient detail, conflicts
373 with other reports or contains misinformation due to different perspectives. The most notable reason for this
374 challenge is that vulnerability reporting has existed in a mostly free text format. With a defined vocabulary and
375 format for reporting the characterization of a vulnerability, the NVD would be able to automate the scoring process.
376 Below are a few examples of how this would be accomplished at a high level. The following description is only
377 intended to serve as a proof of concept until the VDO itself is in a more static and community agreed upon state.
378
379 NVD intends to create a system that will establish this style of mapping through an expression language. In their
380 simplest form, this would be represented as a series of qualifying statements. Some of which would be as simple as a
381 1:1 mapping and others being a far more complex expression. Using one of the simpler examples from Appendix A
382 (CVE-2014-8606) we can walk through the process similar to how the expressions would operate.
383
384 Using the metrics established in Appendix A, we can break this down into the components currently relevant to a
385 CVSS v2.0 score.
386

VDO Metrics	CVSS v2.0 Mapping	Reasoning
Attack Theater: Remote	AV:N	The remote attack theater is in line with the definition for the Attack Vector: Network CVSS metric.
Barriers: Privileges Required	Au:S	Only one layer of privilege is required, so it meets the definition for the Authentication: Single CVSS metric.
Context: Application Logical Impact: Read(Direct) Scope: Limited Criticality: Low	C:P	In regards to the application, there is a read available of Low Criticality and a Scope of Limited. This does not grant any reason to go past the Confidentiality: Partial CVSS metric.
Context: HostOS Logical Impact: Read(Direct) Scope: Limited Criticality: High	C:P	CVSS v2.0 scores are relative to the host device the vulnerability has been exploited on. In regards to the HostOS, there is a read available of High Criticality. While the information gained may be considered of great importance, the Scope is Limited and still constitutes the Confidentiality: Partial CVSS metric.

Now we have the metrics we know mapped, we simply fill in the blanks for the metric strings.

First we will establish the non-impact metrics:	Non-Impact metrics: AV:N/Au:S/AC:L
Then the impact metrics for each context:	Application Context Score: C:P/I:N/A:N HostOS Context Score: C:P/I:N/A:N
Then join the two:	Application Context Score: AV:N/Au:S/AC:L/C:P/I:N/A:N HostOS Context Score: AV:N/Au:S/AC:L/C:P/I:N/A:N

The last step once each score has been enumerated is to establish which score to use. CVSS v2.0 is specifically
designed to score in relation to the host device. In our example we happen to have a Context of HostOS
enumerated, which makes our choice of vector string simple.

CVE-2014-8606 CVSS v2.0 Score: AV:N/Au:S/AC:L/C:P/I:N/A:N

387
388

389 Mapping to a CVSS v3.0 score would follow a similar path.

VDO Metrics	CVSS v3.0 Mapping	Reasoning
Attack Theater: Remote	AV:N	The remote attack theater is in line with the definition for the Attack Vector: Network CVSS metric.
Barrier: Privilege Required Privilege Level: Administrator	PR:H	The privilege level of the user must be of administrator to the application, this qualifies for the Privileges Required: High CVSS metric
Context: Application Entity Role: Primary Authorization Logical Impact: Read(Direct) Scope: Limited Criticality: Low	C:L	The vulnerability allows for limited read to files within the applications authorization scope. Due to the low criticality, this qualifies for Confidentiality: Low
Context: HostOS Entity Role: Secondary Authorization Logical Impact: Read(Direct) Scope: Unlimited	C:H S:C	The vulnerability allows for seemingly unlimited read within the filesystem of the HostOS, this is inherently of high criticality and qualifies for Confidentiality: High When multiple contexts exist, it is imperative to check if there are multiple authorization scopes. In this scenario the Application represents the Primary Scope and the HostOS represents the Secondary scope. When impacts are recognized across multiple authorization scopes the vulnerability qualifies for the Scope: Changed CVSS v3.0 Metric.

390

In a similar fashion to how we created the v3.0 score we will first establish the non-Impact metrics:

First we will establish the non-impact metrics:	Non-Impact metrics:	AV:N/AC:N/PR:H/UI:N/S:C
Then the impact metrics for each context:	Application Context Score: C:L/I:N/A:N HostOS Context Score: C:H/I:N/A:N	
Then join the two:	Application Context Score: AV:N/AC:N/PR:H/UI:N/S:C/C:L/I:N/A:N HostOS Context Score: AV:N/AC:N/PR:H/UI:N/S:C/C:H/I:N/A:N	

Due to the nature of the CVSS v3.0 ruleset, the proper course of action when a scope change occurs is to take the highest rated impact as the score. Therefore we, again, use the HostOS vector string.

CVE-2014-8606 CVSS v2.0 Score: AV:N/Au:S/AC:L/C:P/I:N/A:N

391

392   **Appendix D—Acronyms**

393   Selected acronyms and abbreviations used in this paper are defined below.

ABNF	Augmented Backus–Naur Form
ASLR	Address space layout randomization
CVE	Common Vulnerabilities and Exposures
CVSS	Common Vulnerability Scoring System
CWE	Common Weakness Enumeration
DNS	Domain Name System
HPKP	HTTP Public Key Pinning
HSTS	HTTP Strict Transport Security
HTTP	Hypertext Transfer Protocol
OWASP	Open Web Application Security Project
RDP	Remote Desktop Protocol
RFC	Request for Comments
SSH	Secure Shell

394

395 **Appendix E—References**

[CPE23AL]   Waltermire, D., Cichonski, P., and Scarfone, K. Common Platform
               Enumeration: Applicability Language Specification 2.3. National Institute
               of Standards and Technology Interagency Report 7698, August 2011.
               http://csrc.nist.gov/publications/nistir/ir7698/NISTIR-7698-CPE-
               Language.pdf [accessed 09/09/2016].

[CPE23M]   Parmelee, M., Booth, H., Waltermire, D., and Scarfone, K. Common
               Platform Enumeration: Name Matching Specification 2.3. National
               Institute of Standards and Technology Interagency Report 7696, August
               2011. http://csrc.nist.gov/publications/nistir/ir7696/NISTIR-7696-CPE-
               Matching.pdf [accessed 09/09/2016].

[CPE23N]   Cheikes, B. A., Waltermire, D., and Scarfone, K. Common Platform
               Enumeration: Naming Specification 2.3. National Institute of Standards
               and Technology Interagency Report 7695, August 2011.
               http://csrc.nist.gov/publications/nistir/ir7695/NISTIR-7695-CPE-
               Naming.pdf [accessed 09/09/2016].

[CVSSV3]   Common Vulnerability Scoring System (CVSS) v3.0: Specification
               Document (v1.7), Forum of Incident Response and Security Teams
               (FIRST) Common Vulnerability Scoring System (CVSS) Special Interest
               Group (SIG), https://www.first.org/cvss/cvss-v30-specification-v1.7.pdf,
               [accessed 09/23/2016].

[CWE]   Common Weakness Enumeration, MITRE [website],
               https://cwe.mitre.org, [accessed 09/09/2016].

[ISO/IEC   International Organization for Standardization/International
14971:2007]   Electrotechnical Commission, Medical Devices -- Application of risk
               management to medical devices, ISO/IEC 14971:2007, March 2007.
               http://www.iso.org/iso/home/store/catalogue_tc/catalogue_detail.htm?csn
               umber=38193 [accessed 09/23/2016].

[ISO/IEC   International Organization for Standardization/International
19770-2:2015] Electrotechnical Commission, Information technology -- Software asset
               management -- Part 2: Software identification tag, ISO/IEC 19770-
               2:2015, October 2015.
               http://www.iso.org/iso/catalogue_detail?csnumber=65666 [accessed
               09/09/2016].

[NISTIR 7298] Richard Kissel, *Glossary of Key Information Security Terms*, NISTIR 7298
               Revision 2, National Institute of Standards and Technology, Gaithersburg,
               Maryland, May 2013, 218pp. https://dx.doi.org/10.6028/NIST.IR.7298r2
               [accessed 09/09/2016].

[OWASP-
VULN]
Category:Vulnerability, Open Web Application Security Project
[website], https://www.owasp.org/index.php/Category:Vulnerability,
[accessed 09/09/2016].

[RFC2119]
S. Bradner, *Key words for use in RFCs to Indicate Requirement Levels*,
Internet Engineering Task Force (IETF) Network Working Group Request
for Comments (RFC) 2119, March 1997. https://tools.ietf.org/html/rfc2119
[accessed 09/06/2016].

[RFC5234]
D. Crocker and P. Overell, *Augmented BNF for Syntax Specifications:
ABNF*, Internet Engineering Task Force (IETF) Network Working Group
Request for Comments (RFC) 5234, January 2008.
https://tools.ietf.org/html/rfc5234 [accessed 09/06/2016].

396